Jessica L. Hagan

Adapted for the stage by Ryan Calais Cameron

OBERON BOOKS
LONDON

WWW.OBERONBOOKS.COM

First published in 2018 by Oberon Books Ltd
521 Caledonian Road, London N7 9RH
Tel: +44 (0) 20 7607 3637 / Fax: +44 (0) 20 7607 3629
e-mail: info@oberonbooks.com

A catalogue record for this book is available from the British Library.

PB ISBN: 9781786825100
E ISBN: 9781786825117

Cover photography by Guy J Sanders
Cover design by Edward Kagutuzi

www.bloomsbury.com

To Nanna Pauline Morgan. Strong. Elegant.
Beautiful. A Queen.

Characters

JACOBA

KOKO

RACHEL

VERONICA

SCENE ONE – INTRO

A dimly lit stage, RACHEL's bedroom. RACHEL enters solemnly and sits centre stage. She is looking at her reflection in the mirror, displeased.

JACOBA, VERONICA and KOKO enter the stage full of zeal, attempting to cheer RACHEL up whilst getting ready for a night out. They are singing 'Respect' by Aretha Franklin; giggling, dancing and competing to make RACHEL laugh.

Still reluctant, but moved by the efforts of the QUEENS, RACHEL eventually belts out the chorus as KOKO holds an imaginary microphone to her mouth. The QUEENS cheer her on and they all end up on the floor in laughter.

SCENE TWO – THE OFFICE

The QUEENS disperse into various sections on the stage.

KOKO: If you told me job interviews were created to ensure only the finest micro-aggressors were hired. I would tell you that I agree.

VERONICA: Though we hold different jobs in different industries the experience is the same. It's as if every employee is programmed in exactly the same way!

ALL: Day one!

KOKO: Is full of 'where are you from?'s

VERONICA: With the 'where are you *from*-from's shortly to follow

ALL: They ask me where I'm from!

VERONICA: I say I am a mix. Of both racism and sexism –
they lay equally on my skin

Passed down unknowingly by my next of kin

KOKO: Then they give unrequested information about a gap
year, in an orphanage, in The Congo, even though I'm
from Saint Lucia and I don't like children!

VERONICA: Eventually they ask for my name

KOKO: If it's not English, they reject filling their mouths with
such coloured syllables and instead –

VERONICA: – pick for themselves a nickname – with or
without my permission

KOKO: If my first name is too simple they're confused

VERONICA: As if it's too perplexing for my skin to be an
Abena, my hair to be an Ijeoma, my hips to be a Chomba,
my lips to be a Chinwe

KOKO: But my name to be... Mary.

ALL: By day five!

KOKO: It's 'good morning' to everyone else

VERONICA: And 'yo, wagwarn!' or 'hey sista!' to me

2

ALL: Day six

VERONICA: Can I touch your hair?

ALL: Move!!!

Pause.

Day fourteen!

KOKO: They're snapping their fingers and twisting necks in conversation with me

VERONICA: When I've never done such in my life…

ALL: Week four

VERONICA/KOKO: 'We don't think you're quite fitting in with the team, we think you need to make more effort to socialise'

ALL: Week five

VERONICA: I socialise at Friday drinks

KOKO: They ask me to teach them how to twerk.

VERONICA: They haven't actually asked me if I know how to twerk.

KOKO: I never go to Friday drinks again.

VERONICA: I can't twerk

ALL: Week six

VERONICA: I'm apparently hostile and stern.

KOKO: Not smiling enough but still producing the best results the company's ever seen!!

ALL: Week seven

KOKO: Boss reminds me that not smiling at all times breaks the company ethos –

VERONICA: – he fails to mention that inappropriate, but well-disguised, sexual advances fuelled by your interest in 'tanned' women also break the ethos.

ALL: Week eight?

I conform.

JACOBA/RACHEL: Desks and chairs are stuck in their ways

Computers programmed the same

Lights are flicked on and off and on and off

And decor is hardly changed

JACOBA: Are our office surroundings but a mere reflection of their human inhabitants?

4

RACHEL: Today, I'm tired

JACOBA: I'm tired of switching on and off just to get paid

I switch off hair that grows fiercely in ringlets towards the sun

For a quieter, less intimidating, less defying style

RACHEL: I switch off nails too long and too sharp

Just in case I 'intimidate' anyone in the room when I wave goodbye

JACOBA: I switch off clothes too bright,

RACHEL: Too patterned,

JACOBA: Too tight,

RACHEL: Too short,

JACOBA: Too nice!

RACHEL: Because I can't be seen to encourage the fetishisation that is written in invisible ink somewhere in my employment contract

JACOBA: I switch off period pains and tribulations

RACHEL: Because I'm automatically burdened with being the 'strong one' whilst everyone around me has meltdowns and days off

JACOBA: I switch off boldness

RACHEL: Because to them I cannot be assertive,

RACHEL/JACOBA: I am either aggressive or passive.

Or passive and aggressive

Or passive aggressive.

JACOBA: I switch off my joy

RACHEL: So they can switch on theirs

JACOBA: I dim down my ambition

RACHEL: So not to get in the way of theirs

JACOBA: I switch off my intellect

RACHEL: So they can turn on theirs

ALL: So pretentiously present

JACOBA: Lights on to the workplace

RACHEL: Lights off to my truth

JACOBA: Not an energy-saving bulb in sight

RACHEL: And I'm tired.

JACOBA/RACHEL: Today, the light is off and refuses to switch on

And the office is out of order.

ALL: Desks and chairs are stuck in their ways

Computers programmed the same

Lights are flicked on and off and on and off

And decor is hardly changed

Are our office surroundings but a mere reflection of their human inhabitants?

VERONICA: Like a desk stapled to the ground, he exists.

KOKO: Like a desk stapled to the ground, he exists.

Everyone must move around him, no one must move him.

He is above correction; too reliable to be replaced, too safe to be swapped – to them, he serves his purpose.

RACHEL: He calls Sadé, Shaniqua and Tunde, Tyrone

Because to him we look the same

Because to him they're too difficult to pronounce

Funny how he's never lazy with his mouth until it comes to pronouncing OUR names and identifying OUR faces

JACOBA: He never apologises when he's wrong but expects us to apologise for merely existing in the same space as him.

Like a desk stapled to the ground, he exists.

Eventually he'll be replaced, as the environment progresses and real diversity targets become a demand. He'll be the desk that gets left behind, I hope.

VERONICA: Desks and chairs are stuck in their ways

Computers programmed the same

Lights are flicked on and off and on and off

And decor is hardly changed

Are our office surroundings but a mere reflection of their human inhabitants?

KOKO: I'm fighting with myself to just nod and smile

JACOBA/RACHEL: Nod and smile, just nod and smile, nod and smile just nod and smile

VERONICA: Can I just be still?

Not with fists up or arms crossed or chest raised

Can I,

Just

lay still?

Permission to just be still?

To not fight back

I'm tired

So tired

The QUEENS break into 'Proud Mary' by Tina Turner. They are laughing, dancing and spinning each other around as they sing.

SCENE THREE – THE CATCH-UP

The QUEENS are on the bedroom floor, spread out and comfortably seated. VERONICA is smiling at herself.

VERONICA: SO

KOKO: So...what?

VERONICA: I did it

KOKO: Did what?

VERONICA: Something different

KOKO: *Different,* different?

VERONICA: I had enough, needed a change – I'm tired – need something...different

JACOBA/KOKO/RACHEL: Different!

RACHEL: Help us out, what we saying?

JACOBA: Like coffee with no milk kinda different?

VERONICA: More like...milk and no coffee kinda different!

JACOBA/KOKO/RACHEL: WHAT!!!!

The QUEENS are beside themselves in laughter. They disperse to separate sections of the stage and are now back in their individual rooms preparing for a date.

VERONICA: The night before

Most girls contemplate

JACOBA: 'What hair I should wear'

RACHEL: I contemplate how he'll wear me

KOKO: With pride?

RACHEL: With shame?

JACOBA: With indifference?

KOKO: Will he use my blackness to blind his brethren from his racism?

JACOBA: Am I being paranoid?

VERONICA: Am I the 'wild card' in his deck of Queens?

JACOBA: Am I overthinking this?

KOKO: How long must he date me before he convinces himself he's void of prejudices?

RACHEL: Oh how privileged you must be

VERONICA: To only have to worry

KOKO: About what dress you should wear

JACOBA: And not how you'll be addressed

On a first date.

SCENE FOUR – THE DATE

RACHEL runs to the back of the stage, ready to tell the story of her date. The QUEENS are expectant, invested and ready to assist RACHEL with her account of the date.

RACHEL: He's arrived early!!

VERONICA/KOKO/JACOBA: WHAT!!!

RACHEL: I walk into the bar, and he greets me with a kiss on the forehead

VERONICA: That's sweet

RACHEL: Hand placed firmly on my back

KOKO: Easy, now.

RACHEL: Wafer-thin lips planted on my edges

VERONICA/KOKO/JACOBA: STRIKE ONE!!!

RACHEL: In the process of assuming I wanted his intimacy he
destroys *edges* which took fifteen minutes to lay flat

VERONICA/KOKO/JACOBA: Edges!!!

RACHEL: Which, if damaged, take weeks to grow back!

VERONICA: Must have dated edgeless women in his past!

The QUEENS burst out laughing.

KOKO: Well! I said I've never dated a white boy before

VERONICA: And he said?

JACOBA: *(As white man.)* Well I only date exotic women

VERONICA/RACHEL: Are you serious???

KOKO: I wasn't too sure what continent he was aiming for

As far as I'm aware

'Exotic'

Is used to describe plants and animals

And not non-pale, non-white women.

VERONICA: You would've thought he'd dated enough exotic women to know that!

KOKO: But when you date to feast your eyes, I cannot expect your audio and cognitive to be receptive to the truth! Truth being there's nothing exotic about being raised in London except multipacks of Sunpride tropical juice!

The QUEENS laugh.

VERONICA: But I'll play into his fantasy for the sake of a first date

Aware that by the fourth he'll have forced his desires on me

Exotic,

KOKO/JACOBA/VERONICA: Check!

VERONICA: Sexual,

KOKO/JACOBA/VERONICA: Check.

VERONICA: Wild,

KOKO/JACOBA/VERONICA: Check.

VERONICA: Did he date edgeless 'exotic' women in his past?

Or

Did he never actually date 'exotic' women

Creating a false dating history

Because in his head it's

Make her feel comfortable

So he can feel comfortable

But I'm always uncomfortable

Because I know you're not comfortable…

Entirely.

Or am I just being paranoid

Am I just overthinking things?

JACOBA: He'd ordered my drink just before I arrived.

RACHEL: What was it?

JACOBA: Wray & Nephew with Coke!

VERONICA/KOKO/RACHEL: STRIKE ONE POINT FIVE!!!

The QUEENS laugh.

JACOBA: He described it as –

KOKO: *(As white man, in a bad Jamaican accent.)* A taste of Jamaica

JACOBA: Oh, how an array of insults polluted my heart

As I drank his microaggression

And swallowed it whole

Ate a few pretzels to keep it down

To avoid the word-vomit desperate to come out

VERONICA: *(As white man.)* So what's your favourite song?

RACHEL: Chet Baker, 'Everytime We Say Goodbye'. I love it

And yours…

KOKO: *(As white man.)* 'Niggas in Paris!!!'

JACOBA/VERONICA: What!!!

RACHEL: I choke on my Wray and Nephew & Coke

(There are way too many men in this drink)

Hoping it'll burn my throat so much that I can no longer speak

I'm fighting with myself to just nod and smile

JACOBA/VERONICA/KOKO: Nod and smile, just nod and smile, nod and smile just nod and smile

RACHEL: But word-vomit is coming, it's near, I CAN FEEL IT COMING, I must speak…

So why that song in particular?

KOKO: *(As white man.)* You know I just love the lyricism

JACOBA/VERONICA/KOKO: Oh really? Do tell more…

VERONICA: *(As white man.)* I think it's dope that all these rappers have finally made music that both black and white people can listen to

ALL: Oh really? Do tell more…

JACOBA: We've always made music

RACHEL: You just didn't want to hear it?

VERONICA: Years and years and years

KOKO: Jay-Z's been rapping for at least twenty and he's never begged for your ears

ALL: So there's no 'finally' about anything. He laughs!

JACOBA: Tells me that I'm wrong

RACHEL: That things have changed because now

VERONICA: When 'nigga' is in a song he's not uncomfortable, he can sing along

JACOBA/RACHEL/KOKO: STRIKE TWO!!!

The girls get into a formation around KOKO. JACOBA uses her arm to create a microphone as KOKO prepares to rap. RACHEL and VERONICA are beatboxing beside her.

KOKO: *(To the beat.)* Now I'm feeling uncomfortable

So he can feel more comfortable

But now I'm more uncomfortable

Because you've got way too comfortable

Incredibly.

Comfortable.

Incredibly.

The beatboxing stops.

Or am I just being paranoid

Am I just overthinking things?

JACOBA/VERONICA/RACHEL: NO!

ALL: Nigga is NOT your word Charlie!

KOKO: Charlie

JACOBA: Charlie

RACHEL: Charlie boy

VERONICA: Nigga is not your word Charlie.

RACHEL: He tells me to 'chill', apparently it's not that serious

According to him we needn't get so heated on our first date

Oh what a privilege to be able to switch off from racism

Oh how ignorant to assume I can do the same

ALL: STRIKE TWO POINT FIVE – he's still breathing!

KOKO: He suggests we focus on 'us' and not the world

Not understanding that this is my world

This is my reality

I cannot hide or pretend it's not around

VERONICA: I cannot discuss these things and then go back to my privilege

RACHEL: This isn't a game of trivia, this is a trivial truth

JACOBA: 'Us' cannot exist without you understanding this, Charlie.

VERONICA: 'Us' cannot exist without you understanding this, Charlie oh Charlie

KOKO: There is an 'us' that already exists in me Charlie boy

RACHEL: Being black and being a woman is an 'us' I am already fighting with, Charlie – Charlie.

ALL: This is my reality.

KOKO: In his attempt to lighten the mood, he looks deep into my eyes and asks me where I'm from,

Like where I'm *from-from.*

ALL: They ask me where I'm from!

JACOBA: I say I am a mix. Of both racism and sexism – they lay equally on my skin

Passed down unknowingly by my next of kin

So, choose my pigmentation

Ignore the fact that I am

A creation from God

ALL: Go on!!!

VERONICA: Make me palatable to your tongue. Take me in tiny portions. Break me into little pieces.

Pick at me like you pick at the food of the Aunty who can't cook – selecting only the finest pieces that are good enough to consume.

ALL: Lying!!!

The QUEENS are beside themselves in laughter.

VERONICA: Leading her to believe you love all of it when it's impossible,

'Cus it's *a* taste of Africa not ten…

RACHEL: *(As white man.)* Soo… What's your favourite feature of mine?

JACOBA: I say his watch, hoping that by saying that he'll look at it and decide it's time to leave

He laughs.

I stare.

VERONICA: *(As white man.)* I love your lips

JACOBA: I didn't ask

RACHEL: *(As white man.)* That's what made me swipe right

I love that they're so plump and thick

And that's why he goes for black 'chicks'

ALL: STRIKE THREE – I leave!

Goodnight, Charlie.

RACHEL: Charlie!

KOKO: Oh Charlie!

JACOBA: Charlie, Charlie!

VERONICA: Charlie boy.

SCENE FIVE – GETTING READY

The QUEENS are back in the bedroom. They are getting ready for a night on the town, sharing one mirror between then. They're laughing, helping each other get ready and playfully fighting over mirror space.

RACHEL: I wonder who The Supremes were telling to *(singing)* 'stop in the name of love?'

KOKO: And who Aretha Franklin really wanted respect from!

JACOBA: Was it the turn of events in Tina's life that made her question *(singing)* 'what love had to do with it, got to do with it?'

VERONICA: And if Gladys was offering tickets *(singing)* 'on that midnight train to Georgia' would they have all jumped on?

JACOBA: When Billie Holiday asked God to bless the child did she realise she was deserving of a blessing too?

RACHEL: Or did Etta James perfectly paint out our experience...? *(Singing.)* 'At last, my love has come along. My lonely days are over.'

The QUEENS accompany RACHEL as she sings.

ALL: And we thank Ms Ross, there really *(singing)* 'ain't no mountain high enough...' because black women we just keep rising, and rising, and rising.

VERONICA: Rita Marley

JACOBA: Betty X

KOKO: Coretta Scott King

RACHEL: Stood strong next to men lost in sin, who were powerful and revolutionary in all things – but infidels, unfaithful in the personal things.

ALL: But they're still Kings???

We don't rob them of crowns or hold them to sin.

RACHEL: A black woman sings,

wears a short skirt and dances and flings

her hips

right into criticism, ridicule, claims of self-hate and a lack
of R E S P E C T

KOKO: But you've never asked what it means to me

That your respect shouldn't have a policy.

Clothed black women,

JACOBA: *(As a stereotypical hyper-masculine misogynistic man.)*
I'll respect you a bit

KOKO: Half-naked black women,

JACOBA: *(As a stereotypical hyper-masculine misogynistic man.)*
You won't get shit

ALL: *(Singing.)* 'Chain, chain, chain…' OF FOOLS.

Respect is respect.

Woman is woman.

Human is human.

RACHEL: *(Singing.)* 'And so, I say a little prayer for you.'

The QUEENS run off as their taxi comes to take them on their night out.

SCENE SIX – THE CLUB QUEUE

The QUEENS arrive in the club queue and begin to improvise dialogue. They are visibly happy and excited for their night out and are taking selfies and joking around with each other. A derogatory hip hop song can be heard playing from the club and the QUEENS recognise the song, start singing and rapping along. JACOBA stops singing and begins to acknowledge the lyrics of the song. With this new realisation, she steps out of the queue.

JACOBA: I,

am in love with my abuser

From the streets of Harlem to the Hollywood hotels he haunts me with his catchy words and smooth beats

Syllables and similes used both competitively and creatively

KOKO: I cannot escape him

Even when I want to.

Oh how he varies in flows and melodies

His intonations indicate his location – the West side of him hates the East side of him, the South side of him hates the North side of him

But collectively?

ALL: They hate me.

24

VERONICA: I have always been his bitch

I have always been his hoe

I am rarely his Queen

I am never his equal

But still,

ALL: I love my abuser.

RACHEL: He comes in many forms;

The smooth and soft sounds of Drake – he cheats on me and then sings about it; sings about how hurt he is for hurting me whilst still hurting me,

Profiting from his promiscuity and never changing, he's discovered the key!

Yet I dance and dance and dance to his beat, and I sing and sing and sing to his calling

ALL: I am in love with a sound that

VERONICA: Glorifies

KOKO: Justifies and

JACOBA: Normalises

RACHEL: The objectification, exploitation and victimisation
of me.

I am in love with a love that only loves the light

KOKO: skin.

And is afraid of the dark

RACHEL: skin.

Are you afraid of the dark?

KOKO: Big man!

RACHEL: Are you afraid of the dark?

KOKO: Bad man!

RACHEL: Are you afraid of the dark?

ALL: Black man?

Beat.

JACOBA: I am in love with a sound whose melodies lift me up

And whose lyrics tear me down

And so – it's true,

To be a woman who loves hip hop, at times, is to be in love with your oppressor.

I,

Am in love with my abuser.

The QUEENS are standing on the street, still outside the club and in the queue. They see a group of men catcalling them from a car. They watch as the car stops and the men walk towards them.

VERONICA: Are they coming over here?

KOKO: Better not come

JACOBA: Think they're coming

RACHEL: They wanna think again!

Why they coming?

The QUEENS watch the roadmen make their way over, curious to see their approach.

VERONICA: *(As a roadman.)* What you saying babes?

JACOBA/KOKO/RACHEL: Ahhhhh come on man!!!

The QUEENS become the roadmen and start to shout derogatory chat-up lines. RACHEL, JACOBA and VERONICA gather together as roadmen and stare at KOKO who is standing alone.

RACHEL: *(As roadman.)* Excuse me can I talk to you please?

KOKO: Am I finally worthy of your respect?

Listen to my words and be filled with regret.

JACOBA: *(As roadman.)* So can man get your number?

VERONICA: – I don't want to give you my number.

JACOBA/KOKO/RACHEL: *(As roadmen.)* What!!!??

The QUEENS become themselves again.

VERONICA: And no I don't have a man!

And no my phone is not broken!

JACOBA: And no my Dad is not round the corner waiting to meet me!

And no I'm not a lesbian!

KOKO: And this girl next to me isn't actually my sister!

And no I don't think I'm 'too nice'!

RACHEL: And no I'm not stoosh!

And no we can't just be friends!

VERONICA: And no I'm not underage!

JACOBA: And no my brother is not watching!

KOKO: And no, I wasn't asking for it!

RACHEL: And no I did not dress up for you!

ALL: And no this outfit isn't to catch your attention!!!

Pause. The QUEENS return back into the chirpse.

KOKO: *(As a roadman, to JACOBA.)* Is that your hair? Are you mixed? Where you from?

ALL: They ask me where I'm from!

JACOBA: I say I am a mix. Of both racism and sexism – they lay equally on my skin

Passed down unknowingly by my next of kin

So, choose my pigmentation

Ignore the fact that I am

A creation from God

ALL: Go on…

The QUEENS are back outside the club and still in the queue, still excited and full of energy. Noticing that they are closer to the entrance, the QUEENS are pulling our their IDs in preparation to enter. They arrive at the entrance.

VERONICA: *(As a bouncer.)* The lighty is quite alright B, but I said your girls need to be buff, these girls aren't thick enough! Sorry.

JACOBA: *(As a bouncer.)* They need to be different class. Bodies need to come like an hourglass. Sorry.

RACHEL: *(As a bouncer.)* Sorry but your squad just ain't right. Tell 'em to come back on bashment night. Sorry.

KOKO: *(As a bouncer.)* Look yeah? I ain't being funny but your team are too dark honey. Sorry.

ALL: *(As bouncers.)* Sorry. Not sorry. Sorry!

The QUEENS are turned away from the club. We watch their confusion, disappointment and shock.

ALL: If I cry twice a day will my skin eventually fade

Or will the dark black on my face still remain?

Can I renounce my shade like you who denounced the faith?

When you realised Jesus wasn't really born that way

The QUEENS are visibly distressed by the rejection. They create a soundscape, often overlapping each other with their lines as they confront the bouncers.

RACHEL: If I cry – if I cry

30

KOKO: Cry twice a day. If I cry, if –

JACOBA: – will my skin eventually fade? If I cry?

VERONICA: Or will the dark black on my face still remain? Will the dark black –

RACHEL: – Dark black! Dark black!

KOKO: Can I renounce my shade?

JACOBA: Shade?

RACHEL: If I cry twice a day

KOKO: Jesus wasn't even born that way!

VERONICA: Denounce the faith?

RACHEL: Dark. Black.

JACOBA: Jesus! Jesus!

RACHEL: Black black.

KOKO: Wasn't really born that way!

JACOBA: If I cry?

KOKO: Skin.

Fade.

VERONICA: Born that way?

RACHEL: Dark black on my face still remains…

KOKO: Denounce the faith?

VERONICA: Denounce my shade?

KOKO: *(Furious at the bouncers.)* If I cry twice a day will my skin eventually fade

Or will the dark black on my face still remain?

Can I renounce my shade like you who denounced the faith?

When you realised Jesus wasn't really born that way

Silence.

The QUEENS are still visibly distressed from the rejection at the club. They are especially disturbed and saddened because the bouncers are black men, and begin to address them directly.

KOKO: I looked in your eyes and saw future

RACHEL: You looked in my eyes and saw past.

JACOBA: I looked in your soul and saw King

VERONICA: You looked at mine and saw last;

ALL: Last to your heart.

32

KOKO: Your sexism hurts more than their racism

And your rebuke hurts more than their rejection

I address you with love and affection

And in return I'm subjected to your oppression.

VERONICA: Personal persecution for not adhering to your ideas of perfection

A standard unattainable for anyone.

Black man.

Sorry.

Beat.

Not sorry.

SCENE SEVEN – THE AFTERMATH

The QUEENS are back in their rooms after being turned away from the club. We watch them alone in their individual spaces on the stage as the rejection from the club sinks in. Some of the QUEENS are wiping off their make-up, others tying up their hair and removing accessories. They begin to sing the chorus of 'Limit To Your Love' by James Blake.

KOKO: 'There's a limit to your love'

There's a rhythm to your slang

RACHEL: Inside of you

VERONICA: There's a black man with a rhythm I can't stand

JACOBA: There's a power to your pain

There's a feeding of your ego

ALL: There's the notion that where

(As mandem.) He goes! We go! You go! Ya dun know!

Black man.

KOKO: There's a safety in your stance

There's protection in your palms

VERONICA: There's the idea that you'll defend and protect me from harm

Black man

RACHEL: How did you manage to become my biggest oppressor?

When your predecessors were the successors of solidarity and unity –

JACOBA: – how did you go from finesses of hearts to possessors of hatred?

Angry dispositions catalysing your mission to kill

ALL: Kill my esteem.

JACOBA: Become the spokesperson for 'black women are angry and mean!'

VERONICA: But if I didn't keep you keen

I was a *sket* and a *fiend*

KOKO: I was a 'Queen' until I got on my knees

RACHEL: I was a 'buff ting' till I took out the weave

JACOBA: I had a brain till I clocked your game

VERONICA: I was delusional if I wanted to succeed

You see,

We come in seasons

The QUEENS separate into four sections as they present each stage of life.

RACHEL: Aged one–three years old

Cute, cheeky, gorgeous – strong

KOKO: Aged three–five years,

Sassy and full of personality

VERONICA: Aged six–eight,

School teachers have decided we're problematic before we've even opened our mouths

JACOBA: Aged nine–eleven,

We're sexualised even more,

Told we have attitude.

ALL: By age twelve it's paradise lost, innocence done, womanhood begun.

Because the reality of being a black girl in a white world forces you to grow up, real quick.

VERONICA: Our mothers have made us mothers before our wombs have

JACOBA: Our mothers have made us mothers before our wombs have

KOKO: Murmurs from Mum about being domestic for that husband that we weren't old enough to decide if we even wanted yet

RACHEL: Our fathers have made us lovers before we knew love

VERONICA: Stay away from *this boy*

and *that boy*

and *this man*

and *that man*

Being told to stay away from something I had no desire to be near in the first place

JACOBA: My innocence was snatched away from me from those who wanted to protect me.

My childhood was cut short because there was a hood waiting to devour me

ALL: Our mothers have made us mothers before our wombs have

Our fathers have made us lovers before we knew love

So, ask me where I'm from!

VERONICA: Not where I'm from, but where I'm *from-from*

Try to trace back my strength and figure out exactly where it became survive or die?

Was it when I was chilling with the other Queens on river Nile?

Or when I was forced on a boat? Hostile, naked, withdrawn from child.

Was it when you raped me because you yourself decided I was sexual and wild?!

RACHEL: Tell me where I learnt this strength!

When did it become fight or die?

Tell me how I learnt to hide my fears deep in my spine

KOKO: How the glorified curve in my back – to me, was a reminder that beneath every burden was overwhelming fear – but to you? Was just sexy!

A compulsory feature for the bouncy black woman, she must have a curve in her spine, a curve in her neck, a curve in her bottom and a curve in her breasts!

What if I told you those curves were actually fears? Curved, because the nearer the ends are to touching, the less likely someone could get in.

ALL: Shaped like a U but actually, for me.

Protection.

Beat.

He suggests we focus on 'us' and not the world

Not understanding that this is my world.

This is my reality.

I cannot hide or pretend it's not around.

JACOBA: Tell me where I learnt this strength?

How I could be outwardly tall but inwardly bent,

Crawling on the soil of my ancestral home

Digging my nails into ground designed to give, not take.

RACHEL: Screaming to awake those who had done it before me and survived!

And lived!

And died!

And cried!

And screamed!

And kicked!

And stood!

And sat!

Beat.

Are you really my greatest oppressor?!!

ALL: Are you really my greatest oppressor?!!

Silence.

JACOBA: I take a look to my left

KOKO: I see my sister

VERONICA: Cousin

RACHEL: Friend

JACOBA: A look of assurance dries her tears and a

ALL: 'Me too'

JACOBA: softly kisses her forehead

RACHEL: For years she has inhaled

KOKO: Hate

RACHEL: and exhaled

JACOBA: Magic!

VERONICA: There is a method to her melanin that even I can't comprehend

KOKO: I have watched her decorate life despite despair

RACHEL: And as the sweet smell of solidarity penetrates through walls built from defence

ALL: I realise

RACHEL: I am inhaling a sisterhood that feels less like a fight and more like a right of passage

VERONICA: And through hardship I have enrolled into an institution of Queens!

KOKO: For Queens

JACOBA: By Queens

RACHEL: To Queens

KOKO: And so I look ahead

> Equally balanced by the women behind me and the reflection that stands in front of me

VERONICA: I see me

> In present and in past

RACHEL: I see her

> In future and forever

> *Pause.*

ALL: We even sigh with the same depth

JACOBA: Don't ask me where I'm from.

I will say I am a mix, of both racism and sexism – they lay equally on my skin

Passed down unknowingly by my next of kin

VERONICA: Because there is a method to my melanin

KOKO: There is a method to her melanin

RACHEL: There is a method to our melanin that you can't comprehend

VERONICA: So daughters!

I pray they never have to look past your hues in order to see the human that stands in front of them

ALL: Yes!

RACHEL: Let them love you for your melanin and not in spite of it

ALL: Yes!!

KOKO: May there be no punishment for your pigmentation

ALL: Yes!

JACOBA: No life sentence for being female but

Freedom!

RACHEL: From him

VERONICA: From her

KOKO: From them!

ALL: We thank Ms Ross, there really 'ain't no mountain high enough.' Because black women?

>   We just keep rising,

>   and rising,

>   and rising

JACOBA: Don't choose my pigmentation

RACHEL: I am a creation.

KOKO: From God.

VERONICA: I am royalty.

ALL: We are Queens. And we don't need you to crown us.

End.